The Tortoise and the Hare Race Again

by Liza Charlesworth
illustrated by Kelly Kennedy

SCHOLASTIC

New York ★ Toronto ★ London ★ Auckland
Sydney ★ Mexico City ★ New Delhi ★ Hong Kong

For my awesomely
athletic and super-nice
nephew, Beckett

ISBN 978-0-545-68639-6

12 11 10 9 8 7 6 5 4 3 2 1   14 15 16 17 18 19/0

Printed in China.

Once upon a time, there lived a tortoise
and a hare.

Many years ago, they had a very famous race. Back then, Hare was a big bragger. He told all the animals that he would win.

But Hare lost the race and learned his lesson. He stopped bragging for good.

Tortoise won the race and got lots of attention. Then guess what? *He* started bragging.

"I'm the best at soccer! I'm the best at hide-and-seek! I'm the best at everything!" he boasted.

Years passed and Hare grew tired of Tortoise's nonstop bragging. So Hare challenged Tortoise to another race.

"Let's have a rematch," he said.

"The race should test three different skills,"
said Owl, swooping down from a tree. "Then
you will see who really is the best at everything."
Tortoise and Hare both liked that idea.

Hare worked hard to get ready for the race. But Tortoise did not. He just basked in the sun and said, "Once a winner, always a winner."

On the day of the big race, all of the animals showed up to watch.

"Ready, set, go!" shouted Squirrel.

In the first part of the race, they had to crawl under a net. That was hard for Hare. His ears kept getting stuck.

But it was easy for Tortoise. Soon, he was way
ahead of Hare.

In the second part of the race, they had to walk and balance blocks. That was hard for Hare. The blocks kept slipping off his back.

But it was easy for Tortoise. After a while, he was way, way ahead of Hare.

In the third and final part of the race, they had to jump over a tall wall. Uh-oh! That was NOT easy for Tortoise.

Tortoise tried and tried and tried. But his feet never left the ground. By and by, Hare caught up with Tortoise.

When Hare saw the wall, he jumped for joy.
"Hooray!" he said. "Hopping over tall stuff is
my specialty!"

Then he looked over at Tortoise and remembered how bad it felt to lose. That gave Hare a great idea.

"Climb onto my back," he said.

Tortoise did. Then the two animals sailed over the wall and crossed the finish line together.

"What an amazing race!" said Owl. "You both win."

"I'm sorry I bragged," said Tortoise.

"Been there, done that," said Hare
with a laugh.

After the race, Tortoise and Hare became best friends. They played soccer and hide-and-seek and checkers. And it didn't matter who won or lost—just that they were pals!

Comprehension Boosters

1. Retell this story in your own words.

2. Why did Hare decide to help Tortoise?

3. Can you think of some great words to describe Tortoise? What about Hare?

4. What lesson did you learn from this story?

5. What two animals do you think should race next? Turn on your imagination and tell a story about that race.